MW01286342

In *The Break,* Brandee Melcher recounts her courageous journey - facing a loved one's alcoholism, her own codependency and ultimately reclaiming her own intuitive wisdom. Highly recommended, particularly for those struggling with family addiction.

— MIMI RICH, MFT LICENSED
MARRIAGE AND FAMILY THERAPIST

The Break - Rediscovering our Inner Knowing is a powerful journey into the depths of self-awareness and authenticity. With raw and palatable prose, the author guides women towards the often overlooked wisdom of their inner voices. A cautionary tale, this book resonated with personal memories, and served as a compelling reminder to trust one's intuition in life's pivotal moments. Highly recommended for those seeking self-truth and clarity.

— SHAWNA BURKHOLDER, AUTHOR OF
FIERCE AWAKENINGS

The Break

REDISCOVERING OUR INNER KNOWING

BRANDEE MELCHER

Red Thread Publishing LLC. 2023

Write to **info@redthreadbooks.com** if you are interested in publishing with Red Thread Publishing. Learn more about publications or foreign rights acquisitions of our catalog of books: www.redthreadbooks.com

Copyright © 2023 by Brandee Melcher

All rights reserved.

No part of this book may be reproduced in any form or means. Any unauthorized use, sharing, reproduction or distribution of these materials by any means, electronic, mechanical or otherwise is strictly prohibited. No portion of these materials may be reproduced in any manner whatsoever, without the express written consent of the publisher, except for the use of brief quotations in a book review.

Paperback ISBN: 978-1-955683-80-7

Ebook ISBN: 978-1-955683-82-1

Cover Design: Red Thread Designs

Dedication

To my daughters: You will always be my guiding lights. When I can't tell you to follow my lead, I know it's time for a change. Thank you for your unending, joyous love.

To the woman reading this looking for answers, know that I cannot provide that for you, and I hope you find comfort and companionship in these pages. Know that you are not alone on your path to live your most authentic life as you learn to listen to your inner knowing.

Contents

Introduction

This isn't a tell-all because those don't exist.
There are no villains or heroines in this story
because this is not a fairy tale.
I am not sharing a cautionary tale because this
is my life.
This is also not a guide because life is not a tour.

This is the story of my relationship with love, codependency, high functioning alcoholism and my body. It's a story of unlearning, seeking truth, and finally allowing myself to trust my inner knowing.

Growing up in a family and society that continually taught and encouraged me to ignore the sensations of my body and intuition, it became an act of rebellion and radical self-love to finally stop and listen to my body.

I had to break - spiritually, mentally and physically - away from engrained teachings and the life I had come to accept. I had to break in order to allow myself to feel the sadness and grief that had been hiding behind the quiet anger. I had to break into a thousand pieces so I could begin anew.

This act has led me to *experience* my life and not just be resigned to it.

These are my hopes for you:

1. You find connection. Not in all parts of my story, but enough to know you are not alone in any part of your existence.
2. You begin to recognize when your body, your inner knowing, is speaking up and guiding you.
3. You learn to listen to your inner knowing over the noise of this world.
4. You break and build the life that is most aligned with your inner knowing and core values.
5. You experience your best life.

CHAPTER 1

Family Origins

Alcoholism runs in my family, as I know it does in many households across the U.S. and world.

What I also believe to be true is that many families hardly address the disorder in a healthy manner, if it's addressed at all. In my family household, alcoholism was something that ran in the background as neither of my parents were drinkers during my childhood. There were never beers in the refrigerator or a liquor cabinet I could sneak into. The only time I ever knew of my parents drinking was on the rare occasions they would go out with friends or family and sleep in the next day - again, this was rare, as I have a handful of memories of being babysat or spending an evening with friends or family.

The drinking I knew about originated in stories about my Pappaw long before I was born and my great-grandfather who passed away before I was even a thought. Each of those stories told of violent, irresponsible, unfaithful men, so when I thought of Tim, my then husband, as an alcoholic, the images didn't align with the title, so obviously he couldn't be an alcoholic. He just needed to cut back or change the type of alcohol he consumed or save his drinking for special occasions - whatever it was we needed to do, we could figure it out because he wasn't an alcoholic after all. He just didn't know when to stop.

I remember vague conversations about drinking and drug use in my house, but it was never a major talking point. My parents were more concerned about the possibilities of me becoming a teenage mother than they were of any illicit drug use because that was *their* story. My parents met when my mom was 16 and my father was 19 and soon found themselves pregnant. As the stories go, there were many conversations about what to do with the baby that was on the way. Ultimately, my parents decided to get married and thus began 13 tumultuous, violent years of marriage and family life for my parents, my brothers and me.

Growing up, I was frequently grounded and physically punished for speaking up. The more my parents tried to quiet me, the more I would speak up...until I slowly began to stop. This stopping came after calling the police on my father for the first time when I was 11 years old. I had thought in that moment that my voice had power and that change was finally coming to my home. That the abuse was officially over. Instead, my mother took my father back.

I felt my heart drop and body go numb as we pulled up to the house and I saw his car in the driveway after I had testified against him earlier that day in court. I stared at my mother, dumbfounded. When we walked through the door, he was full of apologies and sincerity. The McDonalds food that had been warming in the oven was heavy in my mouth as I tried to eat my dinner and process what our future would look like. The future I had originally envisioned did not involve my father and now he was here, with my mother and making amends.

The abusive cycle would continue for another two years until I called the police on my father again at the age of 13.

This time it really proved to be the end and my parents finally divorced after 13 years of marital and family hell. Ensuring I did not end up in an abusive relationship was my number one priority growing up; I never once thought about the possibility of loving an alcoholic.

Tim and I met in 2002, shortly after I turned 21 and started dating sometime after I turned 22. I was his bartender and he was a regular. We had a good group of friends who came out faithfully. They had small tabs, the other bartender and I received big tips and we all had a great night. The bar/restaurant scene in my early 20s was a rite of passage and formed some of the best friendships I've ever known. It also helped mask the alcoholism hiding in plain sight. As our relationship progressed, we moved to engagement, marriage and moving from San Antonio, Texas to Raleigh, North Carolina - all the while enjoying our childless mid-to-late 20s.

We would spend Saturdays in a steady buzz - starting with mimosas then moving to Baileys and coffee with breakfast before moving on to the free mid-afternoon wine tasting followed by lunch (with drinks of course) and a later afternoon brewery tour. The day would round out with friends around a fire pit or couch as we shared beverages and laughs from the day. There were moments during those early years that something would happen (a slightly embarrassing moment the night before or an extra large tab at the bar) and we'd temporarily alter our drinking habits, only to find ourselves back at the beginning of the cycle in just a few short weeks.

It was a cycle I began to break as my drinking slowed because I did not like waking up feeling sluggish and nauseous. It was a cycle he found familiar and was content in. Even though I'd feel uneasy at times, I'd ignore that feeling because no real harm was being done and, again, he couldn't be an alcoholic.

CHAPTER 2

Traditional Futures

Thinking back to our wedding, I now realize the amount of compromise I made in the name of marriage and the future I was taught to want.

For most of my life, I did not want to be married. I was never the little girl that played wedding or dressed up as a bride. With the examples provided to me, marriage was not an aspirational goal, despite what society had tried to teach me.

While practicing carrying a lunch tray on one hand back to the kitchen in the elementary school cafeteria, I distinctly remember telling a teacher how I was going to be a waitress when I grew up. She inquired about a future husband and children and how those hours would be hard with them at home. Very matter of fact, I told her I was not going to get married and then couldn't have children so my working wouldn't be a problem. She was a bit taken aback and I carried on, unaware of what a bold statement I had made at such a young age.

Despite what I claimed in my younger years, I found myself young and in love with Tim. Marriage was the next logical step in our relationship as Tim and I had been together for close to two years. In my early twenties, I didn't know there could have been another way. I accepted that marriage was the next step because it wasn't an abusive relationship and we were happily in love. There was no reason to not get married and I accepted the fact that I had to give up parts of myself to make this work because that's what marriage is, right? It's the blending of two people from various backgrounds to form a new version of the future. Each partner is expected to give up parts of themselves, except hardly anyone discusses who is expected to give up what.

Since I was a preteen, I wanted to be married at the Outer Banks of North Carolina - should the day come I decide to get married. I had traveled there once in middle school on a rare family vacation. We lived in Maryland, so this was a very big trip. As far as I could remember, we had never been on vacation, much less one out of state. I fell in love and felt peace at the beach in spite of it being a stressful trip (because everything is stressful when you're growing up in domestic violence). For the first time, I saw the sun set into the ocean and dolphins jumping out of the water. I never wanted to go back home. I remember thinking that if we just lived here, our lives would be better. Our parents wouldn't fight and we wouldn't live in fear.

However, when Tim and I got engaged, we lived in Texas. I had told him when we met that I was moving from Texas to North Carolina after college in hopes of attending UNC Law School. He wanted to come and I didn't want him to come without a serious commitment. So he proposed, I said *yes* and we were married in South Padre, Texas before moving. This is not to say that I didn't want to get married; however I might have waited a little longer had I known there was another potential answer.

For a long time, I unfairly carried the responsibility of his decision to propose. No one asked me to, no one even suggested I should feel any sort of responsibility for it and yet, I did. I felt that had I not made it known from the beginning of our relationship that I would not move with him without a serious commitment, he would not have proposed. Even though he told me many times he wanted to propose, couldn't wait to propose and he alone *chose* to propose, I carried this unnecessary weight. I felt responsible for his and our future. I felt that he would have lived the rest of his life in Texas had we never met and sometimes wonder if that would have been better for both of us.

After the proposal, we waited a little over a year so we could save up and pay for most of the wedding ourselves as weddings are notoriously expensive. His family was willing and able to pay for some of what we wanted. However, I was hesitant to accept most of their assistance. Coming from a family with limited financial resources, I had learned early on that if I wanted anything, I needed to purchase it myself. I had also come to realize during our relationship that most of Tim's family's financial assistance came with some sort of eventual trade off. When the gift was given, supposedly no strings were attached. However, once the transaction had settled and the first "no" was told to his parents on any number of things, we would be reminded of any financial assistance they provided.

Despite my desire to keep the guest list small, it continued to grow at my future in-laws' suggestion because "they'll send you something" and "they're old family friends." As we already lived together and had plans to move shortly after the wedding, we didn't want more stuff to move. We expressed our desire to receive money, no gifts. However his mother was insistent so registries were made and gifts were reluctantly received. As part of the compromise to stop the growing wedding guest list and going too much further over budget, it was agreed that we would have a celebration the weekend after the wedding, at his parents' expense. This would take place at his parents' and was for everyone that wasn't invited or couldn't make the wedding.

This was not my desire, but it was a fair compromise as they did financially contribute to the wedding. To this day there are many items we were given that have barely been used in the course of 11 years of marriage. Many are still in their boxes, untouched and put away in a cabinet, awaiting their time in the sun.

We were married on April 1, 2010.

Weddings are odd events. It's the blending and celebrating of traditions while two people are trying to set the foundation for their new future. *Their* new way of life.

Our wedding was no different, and it was a lovely ceremony with a fun reception full of dancing, eating and laughter. Overall, it was a great day, full of fun memories. Yet, even then, his alcohol use was of concern.

His best man joked that they couldn't let him drink too much, and yet he clearly did. I distinctly remember a moment during the reception looking at him with embarrassment and wondering why he couldn't be sober for this? Even then, I felt and ignored a stirring in my body about his alcohol use, yet everyone laughed it off because "it's a wedding and everyone drinks at weddings."

Yes, everyone drinks at weddings. And there is a limit.

Unknowingly, I was continuing to strip away parts of me in the name of compromise because after all, that's what marriage is, right? Our vows were a witnessed verbal commitment of this. He was moving to North Carolina after the wedding because of me, and so I had to agree to the wants and desires of his family because they were my family now. Only now I realize this wasn't true compromise. This was a slow formation of a person I thought I wanted or maybe needed to be, because that's who society had told me a good wife should be.

Two months later, we were on our way to North Carolina. Two major life events packed into 6 months. For someone who grew up in survival mode and had major life events every few months, this was just a part of life. For Tim, this was a lot as he'd never lived away from his family in all of his 28 years on this earth.

I realize now that I wasn't as kind and understanding as I could or should have been during the move. In my mind, he was being childish. People moved all the time - that's how I spent a majority of my childhood. We had talked about it for months and it was a part of the wedding planning. At one point I remember thinking to myself that he either needed to accept the move or we could get divorced now. This of course was not a healthy thought and in retrospect solidifies the fact that maybe I should have waited a little longer prior to saying 'yes' to marriage.

Moving away from Texas allowed us to grow as a newlywed couple. He couldn't run to the family farm when we got into an argument. We had to learn how to communicate as best we could. The first year on our own was difficult. It took a bit to find our footing and more than once I cried myself to sleep, thinking I was a failure. It had been my idea to move and yet I had trouble finding a job and contributing to the house.

As much as I didn't want to go back into serving, that is where I landed because it was easy money and they are always hiring. It was a lifestyle we both knew well and while he had a retail job, he was still a bar regular. More than once he'd go into work hungover because he'd come for a drink, or 5, at the end of my shift. In our stage of life, this was still considered acceptable and yet it's also not how I was living. Sure, I'd have my moments and hangovers, but this wasn't my daily existence. I would rarely have more than two after-shift drinks or show up to work hungover or still intoxicated.

Even then I'd wonder if there was something more to his drinking, but because he wasn't the rock-bottom version the media portrayed about alcoholism, I couldn't accept that he might be an alcoholic. My body was tugging at me to pay attention and my mind would override the knowing with facts, figures and examples. Ultimately telling me that alcoholism wasn't anything we needed to be worried about and I would quiet my body and listen to my mind.

CHAPTER 3

Family Expansion

As time went on, my drinking habits slowed due to personal desires, while his stayed constant, and often went to excess. We had several conversations about what he was drinking, how much he was drinking, and how we could change the behavior without completely cutting out alcohol.

We were also trying to get pregnant. Going on 5 years of marriage, we felt confident moving onto the next step and adding a child into the mix. In July 2015, I saw the positive sign, and we were on our way to becoming a family of three.

While pregnant, I enjoyed a beer here and there - in fact, the day we found out, we went for a celebratory dinner and I had a pint of Guinness. Overall though, my drinking slowed way down - no more hazy Saturdays or bottles of wine throughout the week - it just wasn't that important, nor did I want to cause potential unnecessary harm to the child I was now carrying. I would joke about having several drinks after I gave birth in the hospital room and that the baby needed to be out by Saint Patrick's Day as I had 9 months of drinking to catch up on, but overall it was not an important part of my life, so it faded to the background.

Throughout the pregnancy and after our daughter was born, Tim's drinking remained the same as it had always been. I was essentially sober now, as I was aware of the possibility of how alcohol could transfer through breast milk and impair my ability to care for a newborn. Again, I would occasionally have an alcoholic beverage and it was usually timed with the feeding schedule to ensure there wasn't any sort of accidental transfer to our daughter.

I also felt the heavy burden of having someone solely depend on me. If I didn't work, bills wouldn't get paid and my child wouldn't have food or a place to live. If my child became ill or injured and needed medical care and I was too intoxicated to drive, there would be legal consequences. If I chose to drink beyond 1 or 2 beverages, it could mean this tiny human life would meet harm. These responsibilities consumed my mind, pushed me to work harder, create a permanent space for our child and live a fairly sober life. It seemed the weight I felt never transferred to her father, so I had to carry the full responsibility of parenthood.

Growing up in domestic violence, I was almost always aware of how my decisions impacted others and that didn't go away with marriage or motherhood. In fact, it intensified. From the clothing I wore to the foods I ate, I was thinking of someone else besides myself from the moment I saw the words *pregnant* on the test.

Science has proven your behaviors, thought processes and brain function are forever altered when living in sustained trauma. I grew up in scarcity. Despite my father having a very well paying job, checks bounced, cars were repossessed and my parents filed bankruptcy. When my parents divorced, the budget tightened, I became a parentified child to my mother and younger brothers and food stamps filled in the gaps. The internal pressure of ensuring our child would not have to experience this type of life was ever present.

Alternately, Tim grew up knowing his parents would always step in and take care of any shortcomings; from financial to emotional, his parents were there to pick up the pieces. This is not to say his family didn't have difficult times and budgets weren't tightened here and there but there was never a concern that cars would be repossessed or three children would split a single package of Ramen Oodles & Noodles for lunch on more than one occasion. His parents were always his safety net; I was, and still am, my safety net.

This is how we parented and lived.

Despite his drinking, he was, and still is, a good father. Tim did not believe in "babysitting" our child. He watched and cared for her because she was *our* child. He was just as responsible for her as I was, even if he was drinking. The main difference being that I recognized the very real consequences of being intoxicated while caring for a tiny human.

As I was working with a network-marketing company (in addition to the full time job), I would attend all day or night events on the weekends while he was home with our child. More than once I would come home late in the evening and find him with slurred speech or napping in an intoxicated state while our infant was asleep in her crib. More than once we would have conversations and arguments about this behavior. I would explain how this was dangerous, that he couldn't do that when I wasn't home and the unnecessary risks he was taking with our child. I was torn between wanting to continue my side hustle and never leaving the house. I finally concluded that I could start to tighten up my timelines, not do events more than an hour away and still be creating an income that would one day, hopefully, replace my corporate earnings.

Prior to our daughter being born, we had the notion that I was going to be the corporate powerhouse, climbing the ladder until I reached CEO status, and he would be the stay-at-home parent. So we maintained our financial state that way and made incremental changes to prepare for that.

After she was born and we were on that car ride home, I couldn't imagine leaving her side as I wept the 30 minutes home. I decided I wanted to be the stay-at-home parent, or maybe the work-from-home parent, and he could be corporate. After all, we especially needed the benefits of Corporate America - mainly insurance - with the expansion of the family. So we began a slow shift in conversation of how this could come to be.

My maternity leave ended after 6 weeks and I went back to work in Corporate as I continued working the side hustle. The first day leaving her at daycare was awful. I cried at drop off and fought back the tears at work. I couldn't wait for pick up time to snuggle that sweet baby of ours again.

The months went on, and even though the urge to be a work-from-home parent was strong, old patterns die hard and newborn land is straight survival. The savings was slowly growing and the debt reducing, but nowhere near the needed balances to make a comfortable leap to a single income household. As our daughter approached a year old, there were more conversations about his drinking and the need to slow down and change habits so we began coming up with rules to help direct and curb the behavior.

CHAPTER 4

The Rules...All the Rules

W hen you don't talk about the family history & taboo subjects, you don't know or realize there are ways to navigate addiction. We began to create and implement guidelines around his drinking. Because again, he wasn't an alcoholic, just someone who needed a little help managing his relationship with alcohol. I felt he just wasn't disciplined enough - which lined up with all the other areas of his life. It's why we were so good together: I was disciplined and had a vision, he needed some guidance and someone to keep him on the "right" path.

Logically, this made sense. In my mind, rules were familiar and meant safety, even if my body felt out of alignment. At the time, I didn't know why I would still feel uneasy about these rules because my brain would tell me this is how we stayed safe. This is how we'd stay happy...and yet, something was still out of balance.

So here come the rules. Some of them were implemented simultaneously, some created out of desperation, some created after thoughtful talks, some created because it made logical sense, some standing on their own.

This thought process is also one of the inherent fallacies of alcoholism. Alcoholism is a disease and you can't "discipline out" a disease. It takes brutal honesty and proper medical and nutritional support. It takes the willingness of the alcoholic to admit they have a problem and need help. **The responsibility falls to them.**

You will want to do this for them. You will force the concern and desire for help. This is your codependency speaking. I know. I also know, and am here to tell you, the responsibility to get help is theirs alone.

Truth be told, all of the rules were made out of desperation because we didn't realize we were staring down alcoholism, so we didn't seek the proper help. It's like having cancer and going to see the doctor about an allergy because you don't know you have cancer. They'll give you rules and guidelines on how to avoid an allergic reaction, however it's not going to solve your actual problem.

If you've ever been in a situation where you love and care for someone with an addiction, some of these may sound familiar and I'm sure you could add some to the list. I know I've forgotten some of the rules we made up because it simply became too much and eventually I couldn't keep up with them...and he wasn't going to follow them of his own accord. To continue to maintain and remind him of the rules became mentally exhausting and I would have to choose between having a delicate conversation or letting my mind recharge from the day.

Most days, I would choose numbing with some other activity or scrolling social media as he enjoyed another beverage. I would sit with my irritation and remind myself that no real harm was being done. I may simply need to remind him to head to bed and then nudge him a little more in the morning to get ready for work.

THE RULES:

Can't drink brown liquor.

Can't pour liquor right from the bottle - it has to be measured.

Can't pour his own drinks, I have to make them.

We'll keep the liquor in the decanters so levels can be monitored.

He can't drink more or faster than me.

No more home brewing.

Only beer.

Only beer in growlers.

No buying alcohol throughout the week, only on the weekend.

No drinking when we go out, only drinking at home.

No drinking at friends' gatherings or houses.

Only allowed to drink when I'm home.

No drinking after I go to bed.

No more day drinking.

No drinking around the kids.

We agreed that liquor was off limits for him. He could easily finish a fifth over the weekend, mainly by himself. The first thoughts were to measure out the liquid so he knew exactly how much he was drinking versus pouring freehand. Then we went to marking the bottle levels and dates with a marker on the label to create that extra visual. Then we began pouring the liquor into fancy decanters we had because they made more noise when you took the tops off and poured from them. I became his bartender and monitor again as I began measuring the drinks. At one time, I was the pace horse to his drinking. He couldn't drink more than me in a sitting. If I only had one beverage, then he could only have one beverage.

All of it was to no avail. All of the rules became exhausting. It became too much to keep up with and they were eventually abandoned because I had enough to manage and I was tired of the discussions. It became evident that the drinking habits weren't changing, so the alcohol of choice shifted to beer.

Much to my dismay, the drinking stayed constant. It didn't help that our local grocery store had now begun selling growlers of local brew. It became even easier to get our favorites without making an extra stop or special trip to the local brewery. In fact, we could enjoy a pint of beer as we wandered the grocery aisles and our growlers were filled for us! I mean, bravo to the store on their marketing and tapping into the desires of most Americans; however, it made the conversation around sobriety even harder.

We were fighting so hard to keep something in our lives that was continually causing pain because all we knew alcoholics didn't look like him, didn't look like our family, so he could keep drinking. The loneliness began to creep in. I felt like I was slowly bleeding out and no one was able to stop the bleeding because no one else saw it.

Alcohol is the only drug we have to justify not using with friends, family, co-workers and strangers...and we didn't want to have to explain why he couldn't or wouldn't have an alcoholic beverage if we went out. We were more concerned about having to explain or justify ourselves, than how unhappy we, mainly me, would be when we came home and he would be intoxicated. For some reason, people can't accept a simple "No thank you" when you decline an alcoholic beverage. The attitude is slowly changing. We can't seem to let people live their lives how they see fit. Instead we need them to explain it to us when it looks different. And only once **society** has accepted their answer, *then* the person is allowed to continue to live the life they enjoy.

To have to constantly defend yourself becomes exhausting so you either succumb to what society wants of you or you hide yourself and stop talking about all the things that make you a beautiful human. All the beautiful things that bring connection are pushed aside because having to defend yourself and your life is too much work.

CHAPTER 5

Newborn Hangover

W hile I was on maternity leave, his parents insisted on visiting as soon as possible. We pushed back and stated they could not visit for 30 days - we needed time to try to adjust to this life. They insisted we needed the help. From the beginning of our relationship, setting and maintaining boundaries with his family had been a struggle. Ultimately, we won out and they visited roughly 30 days after she was born and right around his birthday. We had agreed to do a day trip to the coast with our little nugget while the grandparents were in town. What I had not agreed to was him drinking to excess with his parents the night before, and yet I knew it would happen.

The night before, the three of them had several glasses of wine and cocktails while I slowly sipped a glass of wine - and was the primary caretaker of our 4-week-old child. Again, we were 30 days into this life and still figuring things out (spoiler alert - you are **always** figuring out parenthood. 30 days or 30 years - there's always something new) but I knew I could not care for a child while intoxicated, nor would I want to go to the beach or care for a newborn while hung over.

I woke up earlier than Tim on Tuesday morning because I wanted to be at the beach by noon, plans we had previously discussed and agreed upon. Meaning we would have to leave by 8:30/9:00 and this would work with the feeding/sleeping schedule we were currently in. When 9:00 came and went and I was the only one ready to leave, my frustration began to grow. Tim and his parents were slow to rise and my window between feedings was shrinking. Luckily, we were on the road by 10:00 and were able to arrive just as the hungry cries began.

Since the other three adults were hungover, finding food was imperative. Fried foods were ordered and I was the only one to finish my meal. My husband could barely eat any of his food, nor could he provide any assistance in caring for our child. His parents joked about his state and excused his behaviors because "it was his birthday after all." As if one's birthday is an excuse to forego responsibilities with a newborn.

Look, I am a staunch celebrator of birthdays. I'm one to have a little something special every day for an entire month for myself, as well as encourage it for others. I fully support having a night of a little less sleep and a little more debauchery than routine life allows. However, make these decisions responsibly.

I have learned this lesson the hard way: either by my own actions or being the recipient of others' actions. After making this mistake once or twice, I determined that I could have responsible fun. If there was to be excessive drinking, then clear the schedule the following day and assign a designated driver. If the celebrations were going to be a little costly, start saving a few months in advance. If travel was going to be required, no matter how minimal, set out the guidelines and review them with the necessary parties so everyone can be in agreement. Again, I'm all for celebratory debauchery AND for doing it responsibly.

Thirty days into this new family journey and his drinking

was already making life more difficult than it needed to be. For almost six years, I would continue to allow and excuse this behavior because he wasn't abusive, he was just a sloppy drunk. Here was a glimpse into the next six years of my life. I was already unknowingly deep into my codependency journey with a good person who is also a high-functioning alcoholic.

CHAPTER 6

At Least He Doesn't...

This phrase keeps the bar low and continues to excuse behaviors, erode personal boundaries and diminish the body's guidance. It gaslights you into allowing a life that is less than ideal for you.

It kept me in a marriage longer than it should have.

When the drinking really started to become a concerning behavior, I would rationalize everything and say *at least...*

He's not drinking and driving
He doesn't have a DUI or DWI
There aren't hidden, empty or full, bottles around the house
He was home
He's not violent or abusive - more a drunk frat boy.
It's cheaper than going to the bar.
He's in our bed every night.
He's not having an affair
He's not drinking before work.
He's not drinking at work.
He doesn't have to steal to support his habit
All the bills are paid.
I'm sober so there's always a responsible adult.

We have a good marriage overall.
He's a good dad and pretty involved.
He does love us.
He works hard.
It's not 'hard' drugs, and we all need a vice.

As I was becoming more and more aware and uncomfortable with his level of drinking, I would keep my thoughts and feelings to myself. I was keeping all of this to myself because I would tell myself it really wasn't *that* bad. I would journal it out, go for long walks, work in the garden, clean - almost anything to move the energy and distract myself from how I felt about his drinking and busy my mind with other "more important" tasks.

I would tell myself I really had no reason to be upset or bothered by it because he really wasn't causing any harm to me, the children or the house. What did it matter if he passed out on the couch each night? What did it matter if he had a hangover every morning? What did it matter if he was getting sick every morning? Did it really matter if I kept adding more responsibility to my life? Did it really matter in the long run? As long as there is no abuse, it's really okay because no one is in any imminent or real danger.

When we did discuss the drinking and how it was becoming a bit excessive, that's when the bargaining and rationalization would begin between the two of us. The internal dialog would become real, and dismissed in the same sentence, as I said it outloud to the one person who didn't want to change. Again, because he wasn't violent, abusive or a real danger to himself or others, he really didn't need to stop completely - just slow down is what we would always agree to.

The slowing down would last about 3 months, then his drinking would ramp back up to where it was before and then several months later we'd be back where we had started. All the while I'd be telling myself it wasn't that bad because *at least he wasn't (insert any choice from above).*

I stayed because I did deeply love him and I now know I loved him more than I loved myself or even our children or our future. I needed to take care of him because in taking care of him, I was being a good wife. I was taking care of everything and keeping everything going and from the outside, things looked good. I would talk with close friends and social media acquaintances and feel thankful that *at least I wasn't* managing whatever situation they had shared with me because ***that*** was WAY worse than my situation.

I also didn't talk about my situation with too many people. Let me rephrase that: I didn't ***honestly*** talk about my situation with too many people...well...I didn't really talk about the reality of my situation with anyone. I would share generalities and my general dislike of his drinking. To go into further details or be honest with others would mean I'd reached a level of honesty with myself I wasn't ready to admit. To be honest, really truly honest with myself, would be to admit that there was a much deeper problem. I didn't want to acknowledge the shame that I was carrying. Admitting any of this was debilitating because once I admitted it, I now had a responsibility and I was tired of the responsibilities.

I didn't have the language to verbalize my problem in a way that I thought people would understand. Terms like *high-functioning alcoholic* were not in my vocabulary, nor would I have really understood them. If I had told people my concerns that he was an alcoholic, most people would have doubted me - hell, I doubted me. I couldn't quite come to terms with him being an alcoholic because he wasn't abusive, he paid the bills and was more or less reliable. He was a social drinker but not an alcoholic and social drinking is okay, right?

Despite all of this, I was ashamed and fearful to go out in

public with him, always wondering if he would take it too far. I was on constant guard whenever we were at an event where alcoholic beverages were being served. So many times I thought about not attending or canceling simply because I didn't want him to embarrass me or us. I didn't want anyone to see what I saw almost every night.

CHAPTER 7

The Long Ending

I've been a student of life coaching since I was 5 months pregnant with my youngest. I remember listening to Jessica Butts speak about the Myers Briggs personalities the summer of 2017 and beginning to feel seen for the first time ever in my life. So many patterns, feelings and actions were making sense. I was gaining an understanding of who I was at my core and it was helping me understand others. I was learning to accept parts of me that society seemed to say were not acceptable and let these pieces of me "be".

I was figuring out ways to better communicate and communicate in a way others could hear. I felt like I finally had an answer to how to fix us. I felt like I now had the key to properly share how his drinking was hurting me and us. NOW, we would get somewhere! NOW we could really move towards a valid, long term solution. Again, he wasn't an alcoholic, just a sloppy drunk.

In 2017, before we knew we were working with alcoholism, I implored Tim to take the personality test because I was desperate to try to understand him better. I was desperate to find a way to make things make sense. Maybe me being uncomfortable with his drinking was really just my personality and if I could figure out his personality, then I could figure this out. His drinking is more of a character flaw, not exactly a problem. We could solve this - all it would take is us learning how to communicate better based on our personality types.

GENIUS!

I solved it! Because again, it wasn't alcoholism - it was poor choices based on his personality type.

Not surprisingly, you can't get an accurate personality test if the person is under the influence of any sort of mind altering substances at any time. Each time he got a different result - the only item that was consistent was that he came up as an introvert; other than that it was a guess each time. This new attempt at trying to solve our problem didn't work, so being the Type-A driven personality that I am, I just had to find the next best solution because I was reaching my limit.

Our youngest turned one in December 2018 and his parents were in town for the birthday celebrations. We had a house to prepare for potential guests and I was to be gone the entire day prior for a networking event. I was counting on him and his parents to take care of the house - in fact they had said they were going to do that.

I left for my event in the early morning and they came for a brief visit around noon. Prior to them leaving the event, we had reviewed what still needed to be done, food that needed to be bought and when I would be home. The plan was clear and the instructions easy for three adults to follow. Instead, I came home to three intoxicated adults.

Three intoxicated adults who were supposed to be caring for my one year old and my soon-to-be three year old.

They were not stumbling around, nor would the untrained eye know they had been drinking. However, I knew. After being in this environment for almost 10 years, I knew all of their tells and I knew they were beyond their limits to be of any responsibility. No housework had been completed and yet again it was all left to me. **I was in a rage.** This was the first time I told him that if this happens again, I'm through. I meant it. The ultimatum had been set and things had to change. The cycle had just begun again...

In early March 2019, I called on my way home from a networking event and he didn't answer. *Shit, he's fucking passed out drunk.* I yelled in the car as I felt the familiar pit in my stomach begin to form. *No, he can't be, he had his counseling session today and he hasn't been drinking for three months. Maybe he just fell asleep. He better answer now.*

I tried to talk myself down. I tried to convince myself I was wrong as the pit turned to nausea and the anger continued to grow.

When he finally answered, I knew based on the tone of his voice that he had been passed out drunk. *God damn it! I fucking knew it! Why do I doubt myself?!* I arrived home as quickly as I could to find a fifth of vodka halfway gone on the stove. My first thought was he's been drinking and hiding it in the car because there's no way he drank all of that tonight, there's not. I was wrong.

I angrily woke him up, poured out the bottle and told him to go to bed and sat and cried on the couch while I looked up divorce laws in North Carolina. *You must be separated for one year and one day before you can file for divorce. Damn, that's a long time. I can't think about this right now, I need sleep.* I finally fell asleep and awoke the next day to prepare for another event. Just three short months since I had laid the ultimatum, I was here yet again.

He attempted a conversation and I cut it off. There was no time prior to my event to discuss what I had come home to and I said we'd discuss it later. I had no compassion for him and being around him was the last thing I wanted. As there was no more alcohol in the house, I knew he would be sober for the children for that day and I needed time to cool off. When I came home, we talked after the children went to bed.

I maintained that I said I was done with this. This was the last time and he needed to at least move out temporarily because we needed space. Ideally he would have been gone a month, however we could only afford two weeks, so that's what we did.

He moved out for two weeks after our oldest's birthday because his parents were coming to town for the celebrations. They were made aware of the problems. It was also fairly evident because I was cold and distant from everyone. I didn't want his parents here. I didn't want his mother to tell me to *Just love her boy*. If only she knew what she was asking...and maybe she did, because I believed she had lived a life of enabling and putting herself aside, so this was the best advice she could give. I didn't want anything to do with this. I wanted to figure a way out. I wanted Tim to know that **this was it**. There were no more chances after this. Get better, or the marriage was over.

For our ninth anniversary, in April 2019, I sat across from him at breakfast wanting to be anywhere but there with Tim. I wanted to be so far away from him and yet here I was - here we were talking about how to fix this...yet again. He reached for my hand, as I fought back tears in a public place; I had no desire to hold his hand or touch him in any way. I had no desire to get couples massages. I had no desire to pretend that we were okay because we weren't. I was exhausted. I was tired of sitting here, in these feelings and in this space. I was tired of pretending. I had no idea how to get out of here. I didn't know what it would take to fix this, fix me or fix us. I didn't know if I wanted to fix us - I just knew I didn't want to be feeling how I was feeling anymore.

Soon after he started extensive outpatient therapy with meetings twice a week. We started marriage counseling.

Alcohol was no longer kept in the house and it seemed like things were on the right track. By the summer of 2019, I thought we were back to good and he was sober. There would be an occasional celebratory beverage here and there but there was no more nightly drinking, no more passing out on the couch, no more being intoxicated with the children, no more hangovers, no more rules and no more getting sick in the morning shower.

I began my self-study on alcoholism, addiction and codependency. It was eye-opening for me to see all of my codependent habits. We were a textbook alcoholic/sober couple. There was a little bit of shame as I started to realize my own part in the cycles that continually repeated and there was freedom because now I had the necessary language and knew what behaviors to be mindful of. Now we could call out both of our behaviors in a knowledgeable, non-judgemental way and work to correct them a little each day.

We could get better together. We could grow together. And that's all I really wanted.

Going into 2020, we felt so strong, and thank the universe we did, because the world shut down in March due to COVID. As more and more businesses shut down, there was growing outrage that liquor stores were being allowed to stay open as many people did not consider these as 'essential'. I agreed with this sentiment and I also understood what shutting these businesses down would do for millions of households. To shut down liquor stores would bring America's drinking problem full front and center as people would be forced into withdrawal, without warning. To do that would break the healthcare system beyond repair. We were already figuring out how broken our healthcare system was as emergency rooms, doctor offices and pharmacies were being overrun with patients experiencing symptoms of COVID.

I took it as a personal insult as people were continually

calling for the shut down of liquor stores and the mocking of people with a legitimate disease that they didn't understand. I would have been one of these people too if I was not actively living with and loving a person in active sobriety. If I didn't personally and intimately know the struggles he faced on a weekly and sometimes daily basis, I would have easily passed judgment on those who claimed they needed the liquor store to get through the day. I knew, and while I couldn't fully understand, I could empathize.

So many times in 2020, we would talk about how glad we were over 2019 and that we were better. So many times it felt like we were closer together. So many times I finally felt peace, like *this is it*! *We're FINALLY moving in the right direction. He's FINALLY coming along!*

Then February 2021 it all came crashing down as he came home drunk from going to the driving range and intentionally lied to me for the first time in our 14 year relationship.

CHAPTER 8

Alcoholism, Addiction & Me

O nce we fully accepted that we were battling alcoholism, I decided it was us against it. I had to educate myself, so I dove into as much education as I could. I joined an Al Anon Facebook group, listened to podcasts and read various books on the disease and those recommended by Al Anon. I needed help too and everywhere I looked, surprisingly I couldn't find anyone that looked like me, so yet again I focused on how I could help him and the family, and I'd find my help later.

I needed to understand what this was if I was going to be of any real support. I went searching through all of the Al Anon Facebook posts, hoping to find someone like me. Someone with a husband that simply drank too much and wasn't violent, wasn't a danger, didn't have any real major health issues. That didn't seem to exist, so again, I began doubting myself.

Did he really have a problem? Yes, his psychotherapist said so. The outpatient rehab center confirmed this. I knew it in the deepest parts of my soul and my body agreed. I had known this to be true for years and yet I ignored it.

Okay, yes - he's an alcoholic. I have third-party, unbiased data to support this...AND, was it *really* a problem? Was it a *me* problem and not really an *us* problem?

Did I belong in Al Anon? Everyone else seemed to have it so much worse. In the group where I was supposed to find solace, I seemed to be the outsider. The few times I would post, I would get comments such as "being so lucky" and "you don't know how good you have it" or "it doesn't sound that bad." The moderators would come in and remind the group that alcoholism is a spectrum and that everyone has their limits. I would be directed back to the 12 steps and to find a local group to attend.

I never found a local group and I could not identify with the 12 steps.

Before looking into Al Anon, I began confiding in my Nana about his alcoholism, where I was mentally and what the future could hold. I figured if there was anybody that I could potentially identify with, it would be my Nana. Unfortunately, that wasn't the case. The early years of her marriage were violent and abusive, much like her childhood. My marriage wasn't abusive or violent, so again, maybe I was the problem. I began to feel more alone. And yet, my Nana could understand the loneliness and betrayal I felt and that was a bit of a comfort.

While I had broken the family pattern of raising my children in a violent home, I felt like I could no longer provide them an honest or deeply happy one. I'd tell myself that this was okay, that at least I was breaking up generational patterns one at a time and maybe they could have a happy home. I didn't grow up in an alcoholic home and I grew up in a violent one, so my mom had broken one bond; I could work to break the alcoholic bond and they could work on the happy home.

I know Al Anon and AA have worked for millions of

people across the world. I also know that it has **not** worked for millions of people across the world. Personally, I find the methodology to be based in religious shame and religion - two thought processes I do not support. So just like anything else, this program is not for everyone. I took what I needed and left the rest.

I knew it was a hereditary, genetic disease and it's not the same as diabetes, high blood pressure or cancer. This type of disease has an element of choice with it. While the body may be genetically predisposed or more susceptible to the effects of alcohol, alcohol can't enter one's system without a willingness to put it there.

Unlike food or water, alcoholic beverages are not necessary to living. They do not provide any sort of nutritional value and yet they are a deeply ingrained part of our culture. One's 21st birthday is the official celebration of being able to legally drink - we all know that many of us were drinking well before our 21st birthday and yet this was the date that so many of us counted down to as we aged. We wanted to legally be able to walk into an establishment and order a beer or cocktail of our choice. Why? Because it was glamorized. Everything about the alcohol industry has been glamorized.

Whether being the bartender or the patron, nightclubs and bars were where you wanted to be. I was no exception. After being a barback and a server, I knew I wanted to be a bartender. They were the ones that everyone was laughing with. They were the ones that everyone came to see. They also made the most money. While in college, I had no higher aspirations than to become a great bartender - it was easy money with a flexible schedule.

I became a master at mixing drinks and many times, feeding into people's perceptions of how intoxicated they believed they were. For those who wanted a *strong drink* and I knew wouldn't tip accordingly, they received a half shot at the bottom of the drink and the rest of the shot floated at the top. This way if they took the first sip with the straw or sipped off the top, the drink tasted strong and yet had no more alcohol than the next drink. I'd of course charge the person for the drink they thought they had received and then use the "extra" shot for myself or my friends.

I would employ this same method with Tim, except after a certain point in the night, he would no longer receive full shots in his drinks. By the end of the night, it was a splash on the bottom and a splash on the top. He'd wake up the next day amazed at how much better he felt, thinking he drank much more than he actually did. I knew the truth - for every 5 drinks he thought he had, he really only had 1 shot between them.

In my learnings, I came to realize that his health was far worse than what we had thought. His addiction was actually reaching a critical point to where his health was beginning to take a nosedive. In reading *Under the Influence*, I learned about the nitty gritty details of how alcoholism affects people on the granular, cellular level and how it will continue to progress - especially if left unchecked.

I remember years prior to kids, being in the doctor's office with him to discuss his stomach issues. He has had gastrointestinal issues since he was a child and they continued into adulthood. The doctor was asking questions about diet and one thing that Tim glossed over was his drinking habits. I stopped the doctor and asked him pointedly if his drinking was a problem; the doctor looked at me, looked at him, looked at his notes and said *"No, 2-3 drinks a week shouldn't cause this."*

2-3 drinks a week? How about a day? I looked at the doctor and back at Tim, confused. It wasn't my place to correct this and yet, he lied to the doctor. I remember feeling off-center in this moment and telling myself to just keep quiet.

And so I did, more or less, over the next 10 years.

I didn't think much of it then, but looking back now, the path and patterns were set and we were unknowingly moving down the path of codependent alcoholism.

CHAPTER 9

The First and Last Lies

My body knew.

It was later than he usually came home from the driving range, his new "me time" activity since starting his sobriety journey almost two years ago. I thought it was odd how late it was, but didn't really give it much thought - other than I didn't want to go to bed without saying good night, so I stayed up. 10:00 pm came and he still wasn't home, so I began my nightly routine.

As I was leaving the living room and headed towards the bedroom, I could hear him fumbling with his keys in the lock of the front door while managing the golf bag. I headed towards the door and stopped - my body felt prickly all over, much like how I imagine a cactus might feel. It was as if billions of tiny needles had just pushed through my skin all over my body.

This is a weird sensation.

Before I could make it to the door and unlock it, he was in and was more animated than usual and I instantly knew why my body went into battle mode. **Tim had been drinking**.

As I stood in the kitchen listening to him ecstatically

recount his evening out, I hoped I was wrong, I honestly didn't even know if the driving range sold alcoholic beverages - naive, I know - so I asked. He quickly rattled off what he *thought* they sold. Next I asked about his excited and overly-animated behavior. He brushed it off, stating that he had a really great time and his swings were great and the balls landed where he wanted them to go.

I knew it was more than that, so I asked "Have you been drinking?"

It's a question I have never asked in the past year since he started going to the driving range because, as his former bartender, I *know* when he's been drinking.

...No. NO! I just had a really great time. I hit the ball perfectly, it did what I wanted. It was a great night.

He lied. He lied with little hesitation and I knew - did he know I knew? He intentionally lied. He's never lied to me in the past two years we've been on this sobriety journey - hell, I don't believe he's ever intentionally lied to me in our 13+ year relationship. It's no secret I value honesty & integrity above all and abhor lying.

I tell myself I'm wrong and remind myself it's almost 11:00 p.m. and 5:30 a.m. comes too early, so off to bed I went.

Two weeks go by, and he goes to the driving range again.

It's getting late and my body tenses in anticipation of him coming home full of lies. He comes home late and I **know** he's been drinking. I ask, and again, he lies.

This time we go to bed at about the same time and in the safety and comfort of the darkened bedroom I gently nudge. Staring up at the ceiling, speaking slowly and deliberately, I lay the gauntlet.

I know you've been drinking. I don't know why you lied to me, but I know you've been drinking and I know you lied the last time...I know you, and I know how you are when you drink.

You need to get help. I can't continue to live like this and I told you last time what would happen if you drank.

Silence...then gentle sobs...*I'm so sorry. I don't know why I lied, I guess it was shame and thinking I could hide it.*

We cry, hold each other as we go off to sleep and begin the cycle again. Or so I thought. I didn't realize that this was the beginning of the end. This was the beginning of me holding my boundaries with the one person I always bent to.

14 years together, 11 years of marriage, 2 amazing children, 4 cats, 2 dogs, a house and a decent career - life was good. It wasn't anything exceptional and it was good and steady - typical suburbia. Not exactly the life I had imagined when we married and it was still a very good life.

After several years of arguments, individual and couples therapy and several weeks of intensive out-patient rehab in 2019, I thought we were finally on the other side. I thought we were finally moving towards the future we'd been discussing & planning. I thought the girls and I were finally enough. The cracks in the foundation we had built and repaired in 2019 and 2020 began to grow and this time, in February 2021, there was not a way to repair them.

CHAPTER 10

Soul Break

I had to know why he did it. I had to know why he was willing and thought he was able to pay the tab of his marriage. When the bartender handed him the tab and said, "your total is $6 and your marriage," he said he could pay that.

I asked.

I told him I didn't expect an answer immediately, that he could take his time, but I needed to know how he made that decision when I struggled with buying myself the skincare I love because of the potential financial implications to the family. I needed to know how he could make such a selfish decision.

He came back within 24 hours: *Because I wanted to. Because I wanted a drink like everyone else. Because it's what **I** wanted.*

In that moment, my soul broke. It was so acute and painful that I quickly scanned my body to ensure I didn't somehow just break a bone.

I wish my leg had given out or my wrist snapped in that moment so he could see the break I so intimately felt. I wished so hard for the break to be visible and yet it was hidden within my soul. I explained this sensation to him several times and each time he would stare blankly at me. He simply did not understand and the only solace he could offer was a well meaning, *"I'm so sorry."*

In the next meeting with our therapist, I explained what happened and she said my trust had been broken. My literal trust was now broken and she wasn't wrong. In hindsight, I also think our connection broke or at least the connection I had been desperately holding on to. At that moment we were no longer two people on the same path; we were now two people moving on separate paths towards different futures. We just didn't know it at the moment.

I'm not sure what hurt more - his complete disregard for us or the fact he had lied for the first time in our marriage.

Sure, there had been unintentional betrayals when I would come home and find him drunk after he said he wasn't doing that anymore. His decision to lie was different. He never intended to get passed-out drunk; it just happened as he poured one too many heavy drinks. It was a by-product of his actions - not a conscious decision. I'd like to believe that as he poured his beverages, he never thought about how he was lying to me and himself. That he didn't precisely choose to get drunk, knowing it was going to cause problems. It just happened because he wasn't aware of his limits.

Even still, I was trying. I was following all of the people in recovery, I was suggesting people for him to follow, I was reading books and articles, I was grasping for ANYONE who could provide guidance and tell me this would work. I wanted someone, anyone, to tell me that what I knew to be true in my gut was wrong. I didn't want to accept the fact that I was slowly letting go. I didn't want to accept the fact that I wanted the divorce. I didn't want to accept the fact that my love had changed. I wanted to continue to deny what my body was telling me. I had spent so many years telling my body to be quiet and rationalizing that I just wanted those things to keep being true.

After the break, my body could no longer be quiet. She began speaking up more clearly, firmly and lovingly. There was wisdom she had been attempting to share for years and now, the dam had broken and I could no longer keep her quiet. We argued. I'd rationalize with her. I'd bargain with her. I'd counter her knowing with past actions and history; she'd remind me of what I had pushed aside in those moments. She was here to hold me as I began to accept what I had known for so long. My body had been patiently waiting all these years for me to finally listen.

To admit all of that would have meant it was over, truly over and I didn't know how to reconcile that fact within. Others saw it. They would comment how I was more upset about my job than the state of my marriage. They would ask, am I sure I still want to try. They would try to guide me to the answer we all knew was there and yet I couldn't say out loud. Because to say it out loud would mean that it was now alive and not a quiet secret I could conceal. To give breath to the desire of divorce. I wasn't ready to admit that, to myself or anyone else. It would create an opportunity for someone to witness my pain and make it real.

I remember reading Glennon Doyle's "Love Warrior" and equating my husband's alcoholic lying to infidelity and thinking, "If Glennon could find a way, then maybe so could I." Alcoholism and infidelity are not the same - one is rooted in disease, another in choices; however both alcoholics and adulterers carry the same traits: lying, betrayal, bargaining, codependency and ultimately hurt. In desperation, it made sense. The only flaw in my plan is that Glennon did find her way, and it still led to divorce.

There was no avoiding it.

As my personal therapist had said, "the train has left the station and you are on your way. You can't see the destination right now, and you'll know it when you get there." I knew it. I had reached my destination and yet I blew past the stop in hopes that the next stop was where I truly belonged, where everyone could be happy and I could be content enough.

I mainly wondered how many more times I'd be in this cycle before I finally ended the marriage...because that was the only answer.

It was only a matter of time.

CHAPTER 11

The Shift

Reading back through my journal of this time in my life, I realized I denied the relapse and lying. I guess I figured if I didn't write about it, then it didn't happen. If I didn't create another record of the deceit, and the event only lived in my mind, then it could be forgotten and manipulated to fit whatever narrative I needed it to be. After all, the history that's not written down is the history that is forgotten and is never known as truth.

As the months went on, I continued to bury my feelings. The more I denied, the more things stayed the same - the same is comfortable and if it's not comfortable, it is at the very least known and predictable.

I was too focused on how to financially care for the family that I pushed aside my feelings, wants and needs related to the marriage. I was in my familiar survival mode. The surprisingly effective side effect of growing up in chaos is being able to efficiently compartmentalize emotions and prioritize simply staying alive and functioning. The kids needed to eat, keep a roof over their heads and have their lives as minimally impacted as possible. Tim had lost his job due to his apathy and side effects of years of drinking and I needed to pick up the financial slack.

I was in the middle of negotiating a promotion and significant raise with a company I had been with for four and a half years. I needed this promotion for more reasons than one - my family's financial security was now at stake and so was my sense of worth. I wasn't worth sobriety or honesty but I know I had consistently proven myself and provided value to my coworkers, division and company. I felt like it was finally starting to pay off. I was finally going to get the promotion I rightly deserved and the pay to accompany it.

According to Maslow's Hierarchy of Needs, once I had my financial security solidified then I could focus on personal relationships. Again, compartmentalization is one of the best tools in my tool box.

When I received my first offer and official promotion letter, I was more than disappointed. The salary increase was not on par with the market rate for my new title, nor was it fair for the four and a half years I had been with the company. While the offer was not insulting, it was almost defeating and demoralizing. Almost.

I countered and my supervisor agreed with the counter and took it back to human resources. Corporate held the line and would not negotiate any further, so I had no choice but to accept the offer on the table. Luckily, I had a supervisor that not only supported me, he encouraged me. Unknown to me, this negotiation was the push to the next chapter of my life.

My manager, being just as disappointed with Corporate as I was, laid out a plan that I thought was ridiculous. His suggestion was for me to go out shopping, begin interviewing with other companies and to come back when I had an offer letter. This concept had never occurred to me so I questioned it - my main concern: what if Corporate couldn't match an offer I received? Mark's answer was simple and sincere, *Leave and go where they're going to pay you*. Neither one of us wanted this solution *and* we both knew I was getting a raw deal from Corporate, so it was the best way to try and force Corporate's hand. So I went shopping.

I wasn't fully committed to leaving my current employer, so I was haphazardly and sporadically applying for jobs. I mean the pay increase was decent - it was $10,000 more a year with a guaranteed gas allowance, so it *was* still a considerable increase and I could maintain most of the household as long as Tim maintained a part-time job to cover the remaining expenses.

One of the positions I had half-heartedly applied to requested an initial interview, and I accepted. It wasn't my best interview, so I was surprised when I was asked for a second interview. I realized what could be at stake here - a significant pay increase - so I came prepared. I wanted an offer letter so I could return to my current employer and force their hand for my appropriate pay. I aced the second interview and soon found myself holding an offer letter that was $9,000 more a year and closer to the market rate for my position.

As agreed, I returned to my manager with the offer letter. True to his word, he fought for my pay increase. Unfortunately, the fight included more talks and took Corporate over 48 hours to counter. A company I had been a part of for four and a half years was not as enthusiastic about keeping me as my manager was. I was heartbroken, hurt and realized it was time for me to go where I was wanted and was going to be paid.

I met my manager for breakfast at the end of the week and gave him my notice. He fully understood and wished me well.

My marriage and my career, the two things I had given a significant amount of my life to were letting me down. The two things that made up a majority of my identity were failing me and I had no time to properly grieve or process either of these shifts.

Being someone who was fully enmeshed in a codependent relationship, I was attempting to hold onto control, which is what at least half of us try to do. Chances are, it's instinctual and you don't even realize you're doing it until the damage is done. It's your survival instinct - even if it makes you feel gross afterwards; it's familiar and it's where you go. The neural pathways in your brain are so worn on this path that to take another option in a fight or flight moment, your brain is going to take the path of least resistance - especially if you are at an emotional brick wall.

I tried to repeatedly control Tim's drinking and repeatedly failed.

I tried to force a well-deserved raise with a company I thought valued me and I failed.

I realized I was losing control and losing my sense of self. I didn't know where I was going to go from here and yet I was being pushed and forced into discomfort. I had to simply resign myself to what this new path would be because I was running out of energy trying to be and control all the aspects of my world.

CHAPTER 12

Failure vs. Fraud

Beginning in 2020, I had begun building a small coaching practice. This was in addition to working the full time corporate job. As the world was shut down due to the COVID pandemic, my network marketing business came to a halt and I took this as a sign to shift my focus to building my life coaching business that I had been dreaming about since 2019.

The build was slow, however in January 2021 when I had my first 2 paying clients, I burst into tears reading the confirmation emails. I launched my first workshop and I had people that wanted to hear from me. I had people that wanted to *pay* me. It was one of the most satisfying feelings and humbling moments I had ever experienced. My body vibrated with joy and the tears couldn't be contained.

The workshop went well. I was on cloud nine. I couldn't believe I was on my way to becoming a coach, something I had been working towards for the past year. Then the relapse happened and I couldn't find my footing. I couldn't keep going after the relapse. I felt like a fraud. Every time I'd attempt to launch my next program, I felt stuck. The timing didn't feel right, the program was lacking - I constantly felt like there was something missing and yet I couldn't figure it out.

In hindsight, I knew what was missing. Me. My integrity. My alignment.

How could I coach other women in living the best version of their lives when I was hiding? When I wasn't able to do the same? When I wasn't able to live up to my own mission statement? When I was constantly pushing aside the warnings of my body?

In 2021 my coaching business died before it even got started because I couldn't be honest with myself. I felt like a complete failure. Something I had wanted for so long, I had to put it down because it simply wasn't in alignment with the life I was living.

I had to figure out the next steps in my marriage before I could even begin to help other women figure out how to live their most authentic life. I decided it was better to be a failure than to be a fraud so I never launched any more programs and my coaching business died before the end of 2021.

CHAPTER 13

Rebellions are Built on Hope

- JYN ERSO, ROGUE ONE

This is one of my most favorite quotes. I repeat it to myself often when I find myself going against the grain and finding it difficult to keep going; however, this quote was no longer a source of comfort as we sat in marriage counseling for the second time in 2021. I no longer had hope. Our marriage was not a rebellion. The future vanished when my soul broke. I no longer had anything. I was numb. I was neither invested in us getting divorced nor us staying married. I was neutral to either outcome. I wasn't going to fight for our marriage, nor was I going to proceed towards divorce. I was simply going to exist in this moment because I had too many other responsibilities and making a decision about my marriage could not be one of them.

I knew he wasn't going to move towards divorce, so I didn't have to make any decisions at the moment. I didn't have to *choose* marriage in this moment as I had already chosen it 11 years ago and now it was simply something that was in existence. It was a neutral fact, like the sky being blue or the grass being green. I was married at the moment and I had no opinions on the matter.

Looking back now, by not making a decision and not choosing to work towards and fight for our marriage again, I really had made my decision. I was simply too numb to act or realize it.

As we continued to work through marriage counseling, I tried to convince myself that this could work. We were sleeping separately by the end of April 2021, even though on our 11th anniversary, I wrote a social media post about how we help each other when we fall and that we're going to work through this thing called life together. I remember trying to convince myself that these words could be true and that maybe right now they were not, but they could be - so was I really lying to the world if I wanted to believe them? Was I really lying if I wanted them to be true? Was I lying if I wanted my marriage to work because for it to not work, would mean other things?

We had a trip planned to San Antonio to visit the extended family in August of 2021. I was dreading this trip. I had no desire to go spend a week with the in-laws and put on a show. The trip coincided with my birthday, which only added to the depression.

Prior to the trip, I had been researching rage rooms. I can't remember where or when I had heard about these businesses, but I knew I needed their services. Since the first night of lies, disappointment, anger and rage were steadily, continually building inside of me. No matter what I did to try to move the anger out of my body, it wasn't enough. I needed to break something. I needed to take the destruction I was feeling inside and transfer it to as many objects as I could. I needed to smash things and watch the pieces fly around me. I needed to hear the crunch of plastic or the tinkling of glass as their former shapes gave way to nothing. I needed to continually swing a bat at something until it was nothing more than scattered pieces across a floor. I needed to direct this building rage in a constructive and safe manner.

I knew what it was to grow up in a household where anger was misdirected and poorly expressed. I was not going to subject my children to such a show and so I found one business in the Raleigh area that offered these services, but unfortunately they didn't have any available time prior to our trip. My frustration only grew and I shared this with Tim. So, as part of my birthday present, he bought me time in a rage room while we were in Texas.

After my 30 minutes was up and I was carefully removing my jumpsuit, gloves and goggles, I realized what I deeply wanted was for him to feel the debilitating pain of having someone not choose him.

I wanted him to hurt.

I wanted him to break.

I wanted him to be hopeless.

The next day was my birthday, and I woke up in tears. In all of my 36 years on the planet, I have never woken up in tears on my birthday. I had never felt so alone and empty before. I cried in the shower and had to quickly wipe away the tears as my youngest burst in to use the bathroom.

I had to fake some semblance of happiness as his siblings were unaware of our situation. They were in town to visit and we were all sharing quarters. I was fighting back tears all day and avoiding as much conversation as possible. The less I talked, the less likely the facade would break.

The night of my birthday, he had planned a dinner with old friends of ours and a night walking downtown San Antonio. The night was nice. It was full of hope and we had another great night of sex. The next day, I woke up holding the same hope from the night before. He had put a lot of effort into my celebration and I respected he was trying and yet it still felt off.

I remember holding his hand the next day as we walked to pick up our wedding bands from the jeweler and it felt strange now. Even though it was the same hand I had known for 14 years, it felt like it belonged to someone I didn't know. I could have been holding the hand of the first person I saw in the street and it would have felt the same. My body was disconnected from the person beside me and yet I still told myself I needed to try. I needed this to work.

Where did my hope go?

I wanted to lie to myself in order to save him from the hurt that would come. Even after all of this, I was willing to set myself aside to keep things comfortable for everyone else.

When we came back from vacation, Tim attempted to come back into our bedroom - as had happened all the times before when the cycle was complete - except this time I said no. I said it was too soon. I felt like I was still waiting for the shoe to drop and I still felt like a stranger next to him. I told him that while the vacation gave me hope, he was still an emotionally unsafe person for me and I couldn't regularly share a bed with him.

This caught him off-guard. In fact, he was a bit stunned and hurt. I didn't blame him because in his mind the cycle was complete and now we were back at the beginning. In my mind, I kept seeing a circle with us walking around it - it was like watching a movie. I could see the upcoming obstacles and I would yell to myself to take a different path and yet, I'd watch my avatar continue along. Watching her become a little more dejected and frustrated with each pass. It was maddening being able to watch myself for the first time from the outside and yet it took that "movie" for me to realize I was the one that kept the cycle going. I needed to at least slow it down before I could think about stopping or breaking it.

We continued to sleep separately for the next few months,

taking turns on the couch and continuing our counseling. I was becoming more and more accepting and aware of the fact that we still needed to separate. We had talked about doing a trial 6-month separation and it was becoming more and more evident that needed to happen. I couldn't come up with a date because I knew it would hurt him and the girls, yet with the help of our therapist, we settled on a date and beginning December 2021 we would officially begin to live apart.

Tim was trying to pacify me and do anything he could to get back into my good graces. He held onto hope longer than I did. Part of me wanted this and another part of me wanted nothing to do with him; honestly most of me wanted nothing to do with him. I continually felt stuck in this limbo of wanting to push him away and yet keep the marriage. Not necessarily the marriage to him, simply the marriage because marriage means something in society, especially when there are children involved. To stay married meant we weren't broken or at least we weren't visibly broken.

We had agreed to practice nesting in an attempt to keep this situation as easy on the children as we could. They were already experiencing the changes in the house with 'Daddy sleeping on the couch' and we didn't want to disrupt their lives anymore than we needed to as we were still figuring this out.

We told our children that there were going to be changes. That Daddy was going to be living somewhere new and that Mommy and Daddy were no longer happy being husband and wife, that we needed space. We were still a family and that our family would look a little different for now. Mommy and Daddy still love you very much and Brandee and Tim needed space from each other.

In the moment, they couldn't comprehend nor fully understand the meaning behind our words. It would take time, grace and understanding for all of us to adjust to this new life. While it was what I wanted and needed, I still hurt. Mainly because I was aware of the pain being inflicted on the rest of the family. I knew this was the best option for myself in the moment, and possibly all of us for the future, and it didn't hurt any less.

CHAPTER 14

The Call for Divorce

We had been fully separated and living apart for almost two months, after months of sleeping separately and Valentine's Day 2022 was coming. He suggested we go on a date.

I was caught off-guard at the thought. We'd had some light talks about the relationship, but not much as most of the time was spent getting used to this new setup. There was certainly no affection between us except an occasional hug in front of the children. There were no mixed signals or false promises from me.

As Tim asked for a date, I hesitated as I felt myself internally recoil and suggested we have a session with our therapist to discuss some things first. This was probably the most intentionally dishonest thing I had ever done in our marriage, or entire relationship, however I did not feel safe asking for divorce without a third party present, even if it was virtually. I thought it was over before he moved out and I knew once I was alone I could finally admit it out loud without shame or guilt. I could begin to release the rest of my anxiety and stress.

Not surprisingly, he did not take the news well.

He was angry and couldn't believe I really wanted the divorce. He wanted to argue and barter.

I was firm in my decision and yet, I momentarily considered taking back the request. The brief thought made me nauseous and I knew calling for the divorce was the right move.

I knew it was not going to be easy and I knew it was the best thing for mine and our children's future - his future was up to him.

I was releasing him and my ties to him. I was no longer in control of how his future played out. I could now focus on mine and the girls accordingly and no one was in limbo any longer.

As Brenee Brown says, *Clear is kind.*

And yet, there was sadness. Instead of the feelings of joy I expected to accompany the relief, I felt immense sadness. I had made the best decision for all of our futures, hard as it was, and I was overcome with sadness. Unbeknownst to me, I was beginning my relationship with grief.

I couldn't understand what was happening internally. I wanted the feelings of joy and happiness that I had been expecting, instead I felt a deep void opening that didn't seem to have a bottom.

For the first few months after deciding to move forward with the divorce, I grappled with and learned to walk with **grief**. The funny thing about grief is that it is **not** a cycle. The emotions and mental state that come with grief will come and go in various stages and not at all in a linear path. The cycle is nauseating because you don't know which items will trigger an emotional response - it could be finding an old anniversary card that sets you into a rage or a lone sock in the laundry that makes you nostalgic. It could be the quiet of the house that brings happiness that is almost immediately followed by a deep despair - also caused by the quiet of the house because now you're physically alone and the loudest sound is the voice in your head.

CHAPTER 15

Nesting

Nesting is an interesting arrangement. It certainly has a purpose, and yet if you're attempting to completely emotionally separate from the other person, this is inherently hard to do. If you don't know, nesting is when the two adults agree to share two common spaces - one is for the children, the other is for the adults. The children do not go back and forth, instead the adults are moving back and forth. This was an attempt to keep things easy for everyone else because I was the one calling for the end of life as we all knew it. It was another compromise in an attempt to keep things as peaceful as possible. It was another letting go of myself.

I was a stranger in his apartment, even though it was filled with familiar objects from the house. Not even a guest. It was his apartment and I would stay there when he was in the house with the girls. I packed bags and carried them back and forth. I felt like I was living in a surreal hotel that was filled with ghosts of my past.

I was irritated that my picture was on display, along with the girls' pictures. I didn't want my picture in his space. I didn't want to look at myself while I was there. I didn't want to see his hope on display. It was a reminder every other week of me moving further and further away from us, while he still held onto hope of the future that he so clearly broke. It was offensive how he felt he still had a right to dream or want a future with me when he so clearly discarded me, the family and our future in a moment of self-serving want.

It was uncomfortable being in his apartment because I didn't want to leave and I didn't want to stay in his space. I also didn't feel ready to be out in the world as my marriage was headed towards a slow death. It felt as if people would know I'm getting divorced just by looking at me and I'd be a social pariah - divorce is contagious, if you didn't know.

Yet to sit in the apartment eating endless bags of popcorn and cartons of ice cream was not wise either. I felt as if I was floating in a void, untethered, as everything I had anchored myself to had broken.

Eventually, I began looking for opportunities to leave the apartment and do things I would have created excuses not to do before due to lack of time, funds or childcare. I bought last-minute tickets to see *RENT,* Bon Jovi and random movies. I planned day trips to the beach and climbed lighthouses. I made long overdue monthly breakfast dates with my best friend and walked around downtown Raleigh because it was a beautiful day.

I was finding my way to who I'd been wanting to be. The Brandee that has been waiting to have her turn at life was finally showing up. She was bold, confident, sensual, fun, sassy and full of life. She didn't care if by enjoying life she was offending him. Life was to be enjoyed and for so long, my life had constraints that were simply more than parenthood. For once, I didn't have to make plans for another adult - the only person I had to care for on my off weeks was myself and it was freeing.

Once I didn't have to take care of him, I realized how much I had done. How much work it was to care for another adult. I was learning what freedom felt like. I was learning about letting go of the illusion of control. I was realizing how much my codependency kept me from enjoying the life I deeply wanted.

I also felt like a stranger in the house I'd lived in for the past 9 years. I wasn't able to spend any quiet or focused time in the house by myself as my time at the house was with the girls. It was still considered the "family" house with Tim's stuff all about - only his necessary items were moved out. With the girls staying in the house and the adults moving back and forth, I honestly had no space to call my own as it would take well over a year for Tim to remove 90% of his belongings.

What hurt the most is knowing that, no matter what I did, I would never be the one he chose. Tim could say he wants me, wants my body, wants my attention, wants my affection, wants us, wants the family and all of his actions would still point towards another way of life. Another life where things were done for him. Where not much was required of him. Where I was doing all of the lifting.

I was tired and could no longer lift for the both of us - especially when I thought I'd had someone lifting with me for the past year. For him to drink and lie and just drop me, drop us, drop the family broke something inside of me. And maybe the thing that broke was something that was never fully whole to begin with, just the parts and pieces that were thrown together through my childhood of constantly caring for others and never for myself. I was the one doing the heavy lifting for most of the family AND I was the one taking most of the punishments.

From a young age, I learned I was always an option. I was the reason things were the way they were, I was the problem and yet I also needed to be the solution.

It's an unfair way to grow up and yet it led perfectly to the foundations and shape of my marriage. If *I* didn't have the plan, then things wouldn't get done; if *I* didn't watch my brothers, then anything that happened to them was on me; if *I* didn't remind my mother to eat after we left Maryland for Texas, she wouldn't eat. I was given all of the responsibilities and none of the rewards, only the punishments when things didn't go according to plan.

As we continued to move through the legal process of divorce, more and more items were leaving the house and going to the apartment. The apartment was a small one bedroom and there was not enough space for all of his items. The space quickly became crowded and I began to feel suffocated when I was over there. My body would be tense and attempt to shrink just so I could make the space feel larger.

As more items filled the apartment, there were less items in the house and the space began to feel expansive. Not only were we continually dividing our belongings as fairly as possible, I was throwing away those that were kept for posterity.

For some reason, empty wine, liquor and beer bottles had become a part of our interior decorating, a holdover from our 20's I suppose. Most of the bottles were related to happy times, yet as I went to throw away the bottles, there were only one or two that I could connect with a positive memory. The rest either no longer had a meaning or they brought forth sadness and yet another reminder of a drunken episode that I had pushed to the corners of my memory.

One bottle in particular that I'd been holding onto held mixed memories - an empty 3 liter bottle of wine. We had won the bottle from the local wine shop we frequented. It was a neat win because we'd never owned or drank out of one of those magnum bottles. It's also always fun to win something. We had won this bottle around the time we found out we were pregnant with our first child. As the bottle was too large for the two of us to consume alone, especially with me being pregnant, we were holding onto it to celebrate with others. His parents were coming to town in a few weeks - a surprise I had planned for him prior to knowing we were pregnant - so I figured this would be a good time to enjoy the bottle as we'd have friends over as well.

While his parents were in town, his mother drank the equivalent of 3 ½ bottles of red wine within 3 days. After they returned home to Texas, I remember discussing with my friend how much each of us had had to drink. We each had a glass and the rest was consumed by his mother. We couldn't believe it, so we asked Tim how many glasses he had - zero. His father didn't drink red wine so we knew he didn't have any. I was a little shocked and then we laughed about it and said something to the effect of wishing when we're their age we could drink as well as they did.

Humor. Sarcastic, self-deprecating humor was how we handled our discomfort. It's a natural trauma response and yet effective at masking how we're really feeling - especially when we don't feel as if we have the words or right to feel what's happening on the inside.

Throwing out that bottle, as well as many others, felt good. The kitchen seemed bigger and brighter without the bottles above the cabinets. I felt lighter with them gone and out of the house. It was a clearing of spaces - both mental and physical - that was long overdue. The bottles had become such a permanent fixture that I hadn't even thought about throwing them away until I saw something I wanted to repurpose.

I was looking at all of these bottles with fresh eyes and all I saw was dust-collectors that needed to be cleaned. Instead, I threw them away because I didn't need to polish off bad memories and put them back on display for future talking points.

As much as I wanted to throw 98% of the items in the house away, I knew I couldn't. Our children are a part of this and to throw away wedding and family photos would be unfair to them, so these items were carefully packed away.

As I took the pictures down and looked at my past self, I felt such compassion and grace for this young woman in a white dress and wide smile. A young woman that had such hope as she quieted her fears and concerns. A young woman that wanted the best for him and us, even if that meant she had to do it all herself. A young woman that had no idea that the weight of carrying it all would eventually break her. A young woman that had no idea how her heart, soul and body would be broken.

I told her I loved her and that I was sorry for being one of the people that kept her quiet for so long. I let her know I've learned and that we were on a new path now.

CHAPTER 16

Deferred Maintenance

Being in the house alone after the separation and through the nesting period, I realized all of the deferred maintenance that didn't happen because *I* didn't plan, push, or manage it. It's haunting and over-whelming honestly. It's also eye-opening as to how many other things were being maintained on the outside to maintain appearances while things on the inside were slowly crumbling.

While the outside looks decent, the amount of undone work needing to be completed within the house was daunting. While the house is not immaculate nor winning any Better Homes and Gardens awards, it looks cared-for and lived-in. The inside of the house is lived-in and yet so much obvious work was needed that didn't get done. The agreement had been that I'd do the gardening and maintain the outside, except for the mowing, and he'd take care of the inside...he barely took care of the inside without my prompting. I'd beg to have things fixed within a timely manner or have them fixed at all. I'd then find myself being talked out of a repair because the conversation would move to all of the other repairs and I was left to make a decision I couldn't make because I was too overwhelmed with the general responsibilities of family life. The person I was counting on to help make decisions would simply put them back to me and then when I would give up completely, the conversation would end until it was brought up again in frustration by me. He would take none of the initiative nor engage in the partnership and it was not until I was no longer in that dynamic that I could see what had been happening.

Codependency had infected all the parts of our lives - down to making decisions on household repairs. If I didn't jump over and control all of the parts of the project, it wasn't going to happen; and yet I was too tired to jump with those situations because there were so many other more important aspects of our lives that needed my attention. As I slowly realized I didn't have a partner but rather a co-habitant, the continual control I tried to have on our lives became too much, so the house became a slow afterthought.

I came to realize that the house and I were one and the same and the interesting part is that I didn't realize much of this until my first attempt at dating.

I spent all of 2022 being single and I came to love every minute of it. The weekends I didn't have my children were free for me to take trips and do activities I enjoyed and simply had forgotten about. I could schedule my therapy sessions and not worry about them being interrupted. I could do yoga in a sports bra and underwear, hell, I could do yoga naked - and I did. I could sit in the quiet and let my thoughts run rampant. I could spend an entire weekend curled up with a blanket reading a book. I could take day trips to the beach or a weekend to visit friends. I started having kitchen dance parties again while I cooked and cleaned.

I loved discovering myself. There were so many things that I forgot gave me joy, and it was a beautiful reintroduction. The loneliness I had felt during the last two years of my marriage was no longer a part of me. I felt complete, whole and at peace with myself and the life I was creating. I was having the most fun I'd had in years.

In 2022, I debated joining a dating app. Every time I went to create a profile or even consider downloading an app, my body rejected the idea. I'd feel nauseous, uninterested, apathetic and annoyed. Much like that fateful night, my body was continuing to guide me. I'd have several friends and family members tell me it's just first-time jitters and I should dive in. I knew better, so I waited until my body said yes.

It was well worth the wait.

From the moment we matched in early 2023, everything in my body said *yes* to him. I had three dates set up that week and he was supposed to be the second - a Friday morning coffee date. He continued communicating after the original date was set up while the other guys seemed to disappear after dates were agreed to. The Friday morning coffee quickly moved up to a Monday night drink, followed by two hours of talking, a first kiss, texts on the way home and a second date set for Thursday. The other dates with the two other men were quickly and easily canceled, I deleted my dating profile and both of us decided we wanted to focus on what this could be between us. The Thursday date was just as great as the first and the original Friday coffee date turned into lunch with plans to see each other later that night.

It had been well over a year since I had been physically intimate with anyone and yet there were no first-time nerves. My body remembered what to do, how I liked to be touched, and it felt amazing to have someone enjoy my body while I enjoyed theirs.

We were in frequent contact over the next few weeks as we coordinated schedules to plan our time together. Our time spent together was intentional, relaxed and comfortable. My body felt at ease and comfortable in his presence. I remember having a moment and hoping that this wouldn't end as quickly and intensely as it had started and then pushing the thought out of my head because it felt like a moment of my brain trying to keep me safe.

Interestingly enough, timing wasn't on our side.

He unexpectedly received a major promotion that would consume all of his free time. He was honest and told me he couldn't pursue a relationship. I was at such an emotional rock-bottom due to a week of job rejections and performing emotional labor for my children and extended family all week that I couldn't accept this, so my worst codependent controlling habits came out. Habits I thought I had well under control and had worked through. However, one can't work through all of their codependent habits alone - the very definition of codependency is having another person involved. I know that this was a lesson I needed. It showed me where I still had healing to do and how important it is for me to be chosen. It showed me there was still deferred emotional maintenance to be addressed. I may have looked and felt the best I had in years, yet I still had more inner emotional work to address.

Most will say that I don't want to be in a relationship with someone that would choose their job over me - this is true, AND we had only known each other for 28 days. If I had been in the same situation, I would have made the same choice.

In that moment of panic, it was very hard to see that he was making the best decision for both of us. I was so used to being the one making choices and determining outcomes for others, allowing someone else to step up and show that kind of care was scary and I imploded out of fear.

What was so beautiful about this experience is that for the first time since the beginning of my marriage, I saw what it could look like to be with someone as driven as myself. To be with someone who planned for and took action towards the future independently - without having to be prompted and dragged along. To be with someone who saw the joys and the depression and weight of success. I glimpsed what it could be like to be with someone who craved personal development. I got to see what a potential future with a healthy version of myself and someone else would look like. I was beginning to fall in love with the future I wanted and hadn't allowed myself to envision for a long time because it always seemed so out of reach.

Another part of me came back to life. Dreams and desires that had been tucked away for so long had breath put back in them.

By him being a good, honest person, I remembered all the good I wanted to do and be in this world. Not that I was doing anything harmful, but I was remembering the promises I had been making to myself that had gone temporarily stagnant due to being laid off at the beginning of the year. It felt good to feel excited about me again. It felt good to want to be better again. It felt good to have ambition stirring in my soul again. It felt good to feel desire again. It felt good to see where I still needed to heal.

He was a spark I didn't know I needed to keep enjoying this new life.

CHAPTER 17

Death by a Thousand Paper Cuts

V ery rarely does someone lose themselves in a single moment. It is usually years of slow, small actions that are repeatedly brushed under the rug and shrugged off - death by a thousand paper cuts.

Every now and then, there is a major defining moment. However, when really examined, you can see a bunch of tiny moments that led up to this *defining* moment.

At times, we don't even realize it's happening. In the moment, we may feel awkward or a deep knowing that something isn't right, and yet we brush that aside because no one else in the room seems to be having the same experience. So we quiet our knowing and tell ourselves, "It's just me. I'm the odd one out."

Years of doing this, combined with maintaining the status quo and upholding traditions, continue to push our knowing aside. There are times it will come up as a whisper or maybe even as a loud voice, trying desperately to be heard, and we'll push it aside because to allow ourselves to listen to that voice would be admitting things.

It would be a destruction of a life we've created. It would, in a sense, be a destruction of who we thought we were or who we thought we were supposed to be or who we thought we were becoming. And for some reason, destruction is always met with disdain and hostility.

What I don't think people realize is that in order to build something new, something old *has* to be destroyed. Every single time. There has to be space made for the new to enter.

At first, I think I was trying to destroy our marriage - blow it up by saying I wanted the divorce - because then it could maybe start again. Even after coming to terms with wanting the divorce and all of the reasons why, I still had this thought that maybe it would somehow work out - Tim and I together. And not because I was still in love with him or loved him as my husband or partner, it was always for others. I never claimed I would be happy, I could be content enough and after all of this time, I was still considering and willing to put others first.

I hadn't begun healing, so I figured a full self-destruction would be the next best solution because then I could really begin again. Little did I realize this was the first step in my deep healing journey.

The interesting thing about a full blown self-destruction is what's left to heal is your most essential self. You're now a new being who's learning how to function in a world you're seeing almost for the first time with new thoughts and raw emotions. You begin to look around with a little more curiosity and you don't feel as much shame when you question things. You realize you are new and therefore your understanding of the world is new.

The good news about self-destruction is it can happen more than once and it doesn't mean you are any less valid than the first time. I don't recommend doing this once a week or even once a month, but certainly at least once in your life. You will need to start again and there's nothing wrong with that because every ending is a step towards a new beginning.

CHAPTER 18

To the Next life

Thirteen years ago, I was hurrying towards my new life as a wife while attempting to manage the emotions of my mother, include my brothers in the festivities and keep as many parties informed of the next day's agenda.

This year, I sat on a different beach, notice of divorce filing in hand, full of peace with no agenda or people to manage.

Thirteen years ago, I was excited about the possibilities of what our future together would hold.

This year, I'm excited about the possibilities of what **my** future will now hold.

Thirteen years ago, I began unknowingly, systematically shutting off my intuition and ignoring my body cues.

This year and forever more, I am fully embracing all the messages my body and intuition are sending me with love. Especially as the world gets louder and responsibilities get heavier, continually hearing and listening to my inner knowing will be how I live the next best part of my life.

Every time I feel my body respond in an intense manner, I pause, find a quiet space and ask her what she is trying to tell me. What message did my mind miss and she noticed? What person do I need to avoid or draw near? What deeper healing needs to be addressed? How can I help her feel safe and heard in this moment?

This will also be the best lesson and message I could ever hope to pass along to my daughters in a society that continually encourages them to quiet their intuition. This is the rebellion I am building as I hope they will always listen to their inner knowing and live a life that is in alignment with their most authentic self.

Thank You

I want to thank you, dear reader, for taking time to read this. I know we live in a busy world and our time is our most valuable resource. If you enjoyed this, I would appreciate it so much if you left a review and shared this with a friend or two.

If you really enjoyed this and would like to stay up-to-date on post divorce life and how I am continually coming back to my body and inner knowing, please sign up for my free weekly newsletter at *www.brandeemelcher.com*.

If you have found value in thie book we ask you to take 30 seconds to leave a review on Amazon **amzn.to/482Wn3x** or Goodreads.com. Thank you in advance.

Acknowledgments

First and foremost, I would like to thank my ex-husband, Tim Melcher. While our marriage did not end in the happily-ever-after Disney promised us as children, we are going to find our own happiness that is true to each of us. I couldn't ask for a better co-parent and I look forward to continuing to raise our daughters together.

Next I would like to thank my dearest friend Amanda Caille. You have known, loved and supported me in all my versions since the day I forced my friendship upon you in high school. No matter the miles or time zones that may separate us, I know you are never far. You are my forever person and I am so grateful for you.

I would also like to thank Red Thread Publishing, beginning with Adrienne MacIain who introduced me to Sierra Melcher (no relation) and gave me the inspiration to begin writing again; Sierra Melcher who gently guided and pushed me along to ensure this book came to life, as much as I rethought my decision and tried to self sabotage it; and to the rest of the Red Thread team and community that provided guidance and support as I shared my story and lived this journey.

About the Author

Brandee Melcher is a woman and mother who is continually working to undo the lessons she was taught growing up that no longer serve her or her children. She is teaching her daughters and other women in her circle to pay attention to their inner knowing by taking the time to focus inward and quiet the outside world with tips found in her weekly newsletter.

Brandee lives just outside of Raleigh, North Carolina in her house that is in a constant state of improvement - much like herself. In between raising her two daughters and the corporate job, she spends most of her time reading, working in her garden, going for jogs, and visiting lighthouses in all shapes and sizes.

Recommended Reading

Live Your Life From the Front Seat: Accomplish Magnificent Things in Your Life, Relationships and Career By Jessica Butts, MA

Codependent No More: How to Stop Controlling Others and Start Caring for Yourself By Melody Beattie

Under the Influence: A Life-Saving Guide to the Myths and Realities of Alcoholism By James Robert Milam & Katherine Ketcham

About Red Thread Publishing

Red Thread Publishing is an all-female publishing company on a mission to support 10,000 women to become successful published authors and thought leaders. Through the transformative work of writing and telling our stories we are not only changed as individuals, but we are also changing the global narrative & thus the world.

www.redthreadbooks.com

See our catalog of books:
bit.ly/RedThreadLibrary

 facebook.com/redthreadpublishing

instagram.com/redthreadbooks

Made in the USA
Middletown, DE
05 November 2023

41817842R00061